DATE: _____ TIME: _____

WEATHER: _____

TODAY I FEEL...

_____
_____
_____
_____

I AM EXCITED ABOUT...

_____
_____
_____
_____

I AM CONCERNED ABOUT...

_____
_____
_____
_____

SOMETHING OR SOMEONE THAT BRIGHTENED MY DAY...

WHAT HAPPENED TODAY...

_____
_____
_____
_____
_____
_____

WHAT I MISS MOST...

_____
_____
_____
_____

THINGS I CAN'T WAIT TO SHARE...

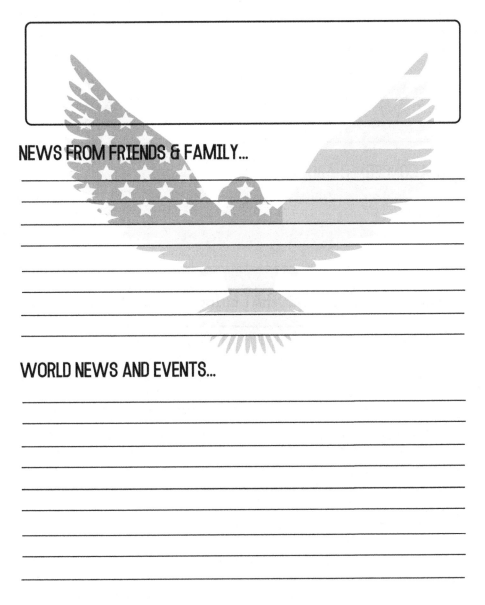

NEWS FROM FRIENDS & FAMILY...

_____
_____
_____
_____
_____
_____
_____

WORLD NEWS AND EVENTS...

_____
_____
_____
_____
_____
_____
_____
_____

DATE: _____ TIME: _____

WEATHER: _____

TODAY I FEEL...

_____
_____
_____
_____

I AM EXCITED ABOUT...

_____
_____
_____

I AM CONCERNED ABOUT...

_____
_____
_____

SOMETHING OR SOMEONE THAT BRIGHTENED MY DAY...

WHAT HAPPENED TODAY...

_____
_____
_____
_____
_____

WHAT I MISS MOST...

_____
_____
_____
_____
_____

THINGS I CAN'T WAIT TO SHARE...

NEWS FROM FRIENDS & FAMILY...

_____
_____
_____
_____
_____
_____
_____
_____

WORLD NEWS AND EVENTS...

_____
_____
_____
_____
_____
_____
_____
_____
_____
_____

DATE: _____   TIME: _____

WEATHER: _____

TODAY I FEEL...
_____
_____
_____
_____

I AM EXCITED ABOUT...
_____
_____
_____

I AM CONCERNED ABOUT...
_____
_____
_____
_____

SOMETHING OR SOMEONE THAT BRIGHTENED MY DAY...

WHAT HAPPENED TODAY...
_____
_____
_____
_____
_____
_____

WHAT I MISS MOST...

_____
_____
_____
_____

THINGS I CAN'T WAIT TO SHARE...

NEWS FROM FRIENDS & FAMILY...

_____
_____
_____
_____
_____
_____
_____

WORLD NEWS AND EVENTS...

_____
_____
_____
_____
_____
_____
_____
_____
_____

DATE: _____ TIME: _____

WEATHER: _____

TODAY I FEEL...

_____
_____
_____
_____

I AM EXCITED ABOUT...

_____
_____
_____
_____

I AM CONCERNED ABOUT...

_____
_____
_____
_____

SOMETHING OR SOMEONE THAT BRIGHTENED MY DAY...

WHAT HAPPENED TODAY...

_____
_____
_____
_____
_____

WHAT I MISS MOST...

_____
_____
_____
_____

THINGS I CAN'T WAIT TO SHARE...

NEWS FROM FRIENDS & FAMILY...

_____
_____
_____
_____
_____
_____
_____

WORLD NEWS AND EVENTS...

_____
_____
_____
_____
_____
_____
_____
_____
_____

DATE: _____ TIME: _____

WEATHER: _____

TODAY I FEEL...

_____
_____
_____
_____
_____

I AM EXCITED ABOUT...

_____
_____
_____
_____

I AM CONCERNED ABOUT...

_____
_____
_____
_____

SOMETHING OR SOMEONE THAT BRIGHTENED MY DAY...

WHAT HAPPENED TODAY...

_____
_____
_____
_____
_____
_____

WHAT I MISS MOST...

_____
_____
_____
_____

THINGS I CAN'T WAIT TO SHARE...

NEWS FROM FRIENDS & FAMILY...

_____
_____
_____
_____
_____
_____

WORLD NEWS AND EVENTS...

_____
_____
_____
_____
_____
_____
_____
_____

DATE: _____ TIME: _____

WEATHER: _____

TODAY I FEEL...

_____
_____
_____
_____

I AM EXCITED ABOUT...

_____
_____
_____
_____

I AM CONCERNED ABOUT...

_____
_____
_____
_____

SOMETHING OR SOMEONE THAT BRIGHTENED MY DAY...

WHAT HAPPENED TODAY...

_____
_____
_____
_____
_____
_____

WHAT I MISS MOST...

_____
_____
_____
_____

THINGS I CAN'T WAIT TO SHARE...

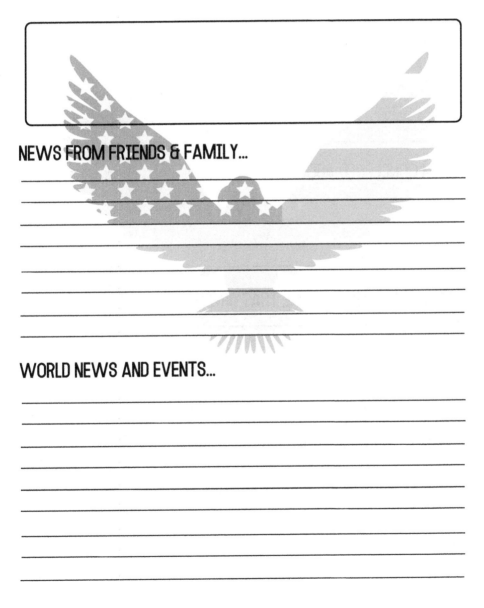

NEWS FROM FRIENDS & FAMILY...

_____
_____
_____
_____
_____
_____
_____

WORLD NEWS AND EVENTS...

_____
_____
_____
_____
_____
_____
_____
_____
_____

DATE: _____ TIME: _____

WEATHER: _____

TODAY I FEEL...

_____
_____
_____
_____

I AM EXCITED ABOUT...

_____
_____
_____

I AM CONCERNED ABOUT...

_____
_____
_____

SOMETHING OR SOMEONE THAT BRIGHTENED MY DAY...

WHAT HAPPENED TODAY...

_____
_____
_____
_____
_____
_____

WHAT I MISS MOST...

_____
_____
_____
_____

THINGS I CAN'T WAIT TO SHARE...

NEWS FROM FRIENDS & FAMILY...

_____
_____
_____
_____
_____
_____
_____

WORLD NEWS AND EVENTS...

_____
_____
_____
_____
_____
_____
_____
_____
_____

DATE: _____ TIME: _____

WEATHER: _____

TODAY I FEEL...

_____
_____
_____
_____

I AM EXCITED ABOUT...

_____
_____
_____
_____

I AM CONCERNED ABOUT...

_____
_____
_____
_____

SOMETHING OR SOMEONE THAT BRIGHTENED MY DAY...

WHAT HAPPENED TODAY...

_____
_____
_____
_____
_____
_____

WHAT I MISS MOST...

_____
_____
_____
_____

THINGS I CAN'T WAIT TO SHARE...

NEWS FROM FRIENDS & FAMILY...

_____
_____
_____
_____
_____
_____
_____

WORLD NEWS AND EVENTS...

_____
_____
_____
_____
_____
_____
_____
_____
_____

DATE: _____   TIME: _____

WEATHER: _____

TODAY I FEEL...
_____
_____
_____
_____

I AM EXCITED ABOUT...
_____
_____
_____
_____

I AM CONCERNED ABOUT...
_____
_____
_____
_____

SOMETHING OR SOMEONE THAT BRIGHTENED MY DAY...

WHAT HAPPENED TODAY...
_____
_____
_____
_____
_____
_____

WHAT I MISS MOST...

_____
_____
_____
_____

THINGS I CAN'T WAIT TO SHARE...

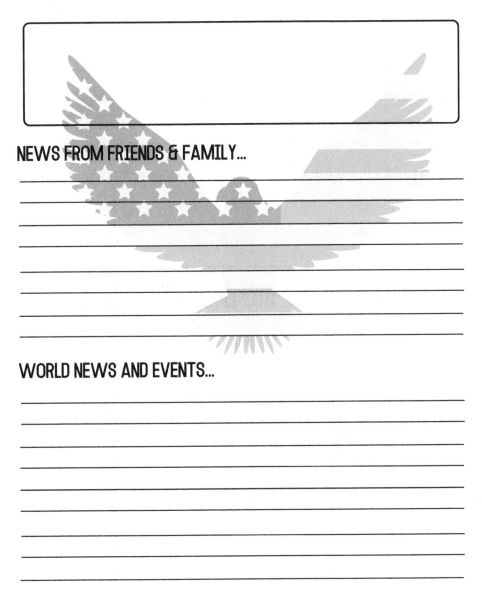

NEWS FROM FRIENDS & FAMILY...

_____
_____
_____
_____
_____
_____
_____

WORLD NEWS AND EVENTS...

_____
_____
_____
_____
_____
_____
_____
_____

DATE: _____ TIME: _____

WEATHER: _____

TODAY I FEEL...

_____
_____
_____
_____

I AM EXCITED ABOUT...

_____
_____
_____

I AM CONCERNED ABOUT...

_____
_____
_____
_____

SOMETHING OR SOMEONE THAT BRIGHTENED MY DAY...

WHAT HAPPENED TODAY...

_____
_____
_____
_____
_____

WHAT I MISS MOST...

_____
_____
_____
_____

THINGS I CAN'T WAIT TO SHARE...

NEWS FROM FRIENDS & FAMILY...

_____
_____
_____
_____
_____
_____
_____

WORLD NEWS AND EVENTS...

_____
_____
_____
_____
_____
_____
_____
_____
_____
_____

DATE: _____ TIME: _____

WEATHER: _____

TODAY I FEEL...

_____
_____
_____
_____

I AM EXCITED ABOUT...

_____
_____
_____

I AM CONCERNED ABOUT...

_____
_____
_____
_____

SOMETHING OR SOMEONE THAT BRIGHTENED MY DAY...

WHAT HAPPENED TODAY...

_____
_____
_____
_____
_____
_____

WHAT I MISS MOST...

_____
_____
_____
_____

THINGS I CAN'T WAIT TO SHARE...

NEWS FROM FRIENDS & FAMILY...

_____
_____
_____
_____
_____
_____
_____

WORLD NEWS AND EVENTS...

_____
_____
_____
_____
_____
_____
_____
_____

DATE: _____ TIME: _____

WEATHER: _____

TODAY I FEEL...

_____
_____
_____
_____

I AM EXCITED ABOUT...

_____
_____
_____

I AM CONCERNED ABOUT...

_____
_____
_____
_____

SOMETHING OR SOMEONE THAT BRIGHTENED MY DAY...

WHAT HAPPENED TODAY...

_____
_____
_____
_____
_____
_____

WHAT I MISS MOST...

_____
_____
_____
_____

THINGS I CAN'T WAIT TO SHARE...

NEWS FROM FRIENDS & FAMILY...

_____
_____
_____
_____
_____
_____
_____

WORLD NEWS AND EVENTS...

_____
_____
_____
_____
_____
_____
_____
_____
_____

DATE: _____   TIME: _____

WEATHER: _____

TODAY I FEEL...

_____
_____
_____
_____

I AM EXCITED ABOUT...

_____
_____
_____
_____

I AM CONCERNED ABOUT...

_____
_____
_____
_____

SOMETHING OR SOMEONE THAT BRIGHTENED MY DAY...

WHAT HAPPENED TODAY...

_____
_____
_____
_____
_____

WHAT I MISS MOST...

THINGS I CAN'T WAIT TO SHARE...

NEWS FROM FRIENDS & FAMILY...

WORLD NEWS AND EVENTS...

DATE: _____   TIME: _____

WEATHER: _____

TODAY I FEEL...

_____
_____
_____
_____

I AM EXCITED ABOUT...

_____
_____
_____
_____

I AM CONCERNED ABOUT...

_____
_____
_____
_____

SOMETHING OR SOMEONE THAT BRIGHTENED MY DAY...

WHAT HAPPENED TODAY...

_____
_____
_____
_____
_____
_____

WHAT I MISS MOST...

_____
_____
_____
_____

THINGS I CAN'T WAIT TO SHARE...

NEWS FROM FRIENDS & FAMILY...

_____
_____
_____
_____
_____
_____

WORLD NEWS AND EVENTS...

_____
_____
_____
_____
_____
_____
_____
_____

DATE: _____ TIME: _____

WEATHER: _____

TODAY I FEEL...
_____
_____
_____
_____

I AM EXCITED ABOUT...
_____
_____
_____
_____

I AM CONCERNED ABOUT...
_____
_____
_____
_____

SOMETHING OR SOMEONE THAT BRIGHTENED MY DAY...

WHAT HAPPENED TODAY...
_____
_____
_____
_____
_____
_____

WHAT I MISS MOST...

_____
_____
_____
_____

THINGS I CAN'T WAIT TO SHARE...

NEWS FROM FRIENDS & FAMILY...

_____
_____
_____
_____
_____
_____
_____

WORLD NEWS AND EVENTS...

_____
_____
_____
_____
_____
_____
_____
_____
_____

DATE: _____ TIME: _____

WEATHER: _____

TODAY I FEEL...

_____
_____
_____
_____

I AM EXCITED ABOUT...

_____
_____
_____
_____

I AM CONCERNED ABOUT...

_____
_____
_____
_____

SOMETHING OR SOMEONE THAT BRIGHTENED MY DAY...

WHAT HAPPENED TODAY...

_____
_____
_____
_____
_____
_____

WHAT I MISS MOST...

_____
_____
_____
_____

THINGS I CAN'T WAIT TO SHARE...

NEWS FROM FRIENDS & FAMILY...

_____
_____
_____
_____
_____
_____

WORLD NEWS AND EVENTS...

_____
_____
_____
_____
_____
_____
_____
_____
_____

DATE: _____   TIME: _____

WEATHER: _____

TODAY I FEEL...
_____
_____
_____
_____

I AM EXCITED ABOUT...
_____
_____
_____
_____

I AM CONCERNED ABOUT...
_____
_____
_____
_____

SOMETHING OR SOMEONE THAT BRIGHTENED MY DAY...

WHAT HAPPENED TODAY...
_____
_____
_____
_____
_____
_____

WHAT I MISS MOST...

_____
_____
_____
_____

THINGS I CAN'T WAIT TO SHARE...

NEWS FROM FRIENDS & FAMILY...

_____
_____
_____
_____
_____
_____
_____

WORLD NEWS AND EVENTS...

_____
_____
_____
_____
_____
_____
_____
_____

DATE: _____   TIME: _____

WEATHER: _____

TODAY I FEEL...
_____
_____
_____
_____

I AM EXCITED ABOUT...
_____
_____
_____
_____

I AM CONCERNED ABOUT...
_____
_____
_____
_____

SOMETHING OR SOMEONE THAT BRIGHTENED MY DAY...

WHAT HAPPENED TODAY...
_____
_____
_____
_____
_____
_____

WHAT I MISS MOST...

_____
_____
_____
_____

THINGS I CAN'T WAIT TO SHARE...

NEWS FROM FRIENDS & FAMILY...

_____
_____
_____
_____
_____
_____
_____

WORLD NEWS AND EVENTS...

_____
_____
_____
_____
_____
_____
_____
_____
_____

DATE: _____   TIME: _____

WEATHER: _____

TODAY I FEEL...

_____
_____
_____
_____

I AM EXCITED ABOUT...

_____
_____
_____
_____

I AM CONCERNED ABOUT...

_____
_____
_____
_____

SOMETHING OR SOMEONE THAT BRIGHTENED MY DAY...

WHAT HAPPENED TODAY...

_____
_____
_____
_____
_____
_____

WHAT I MISS MOST...

_____
_____
_____
_____

THINGS I CAN'T WAIT TO SHARE...

NEWS FROM FRIENDS & FAMILY...

_____
_____
_____
_____
_____
_____

WORLD NEWS AND EVENTS...

_____
_____
_____
_____
_____
_____
_____
_____

DATE: _____ TIME: _____

WEATHER: _____

TODAY I FEEL...
_____
_____
_____
_____

I AM EXCITED ABOUT...
_____
_____
_____

I AM CONCERNED ABOUT...
_____
_____
_____
_____

SOMETHING OR SOMEONE THAT BRIGHTENED MY DAY...

WHAT HAPPENED TODAY...
_____
_____
_____
_____
_____
_____

WHAT I MISS MOST...

_____
_____
_____
_____

THINGS I CAN'T WAIT TO SHARE...

NEWS FROM FRIENDS & FAMILY...

_____
_____
_____
_____
_____
_____

WORLD NEWS AND EVENTS...

_____
_____
_____
_____
_____
_____
_____
_____

DATE: _____   TIME: _____

WEATHER: _____

TODAY I FEEL...

_____
_____
_____
_____

I AM EXCITED ABOUT...

_____
_____
_____

I AM CONCERNED ABOUT...

_____
_____
_____
_____

SOMETHING OR SOMEONE THAT BRIGHTENED MY DAY...

WHAT HAPPENED TODAY...

_____
_____
_____
_____
_____
_____

WHAT I MISS MOST...

_____
_____
_____
_____

THINGS I CAN'T WAIT TO SHARE...

NEWS FROM FRIENDS & FAMILY...

_____
_____
_____
_____
_____
_____
_____

WORLD NEWS AND EVENTS...

_____
_____
_____
_____
_____
_____
_____
_____

DATE: _____ TIME: _____

WEATHER: _____

TODAY I FEEL...

_____
_____
_____
_____

I AM EXCITED ABOUT...

_____
_____
_____
_____

I AM CONCERNED ABOUT...

_____
_____
_____
_____

SOMETHING OR SOMEONE THAT BRIGHTENED MY DAY...

WHAT HAPPENED TODAY...

_____
_____
_____
_____
_____
_____

WHAT I MISS MOST...

_____

_____

_____

_____

THINGS I CAN'T WAIT TO SHARE...

NEWS FROM FRIENDS & FAMILY...

_____

_____

_____

_____

_____

_____

_____

WORLD NEWS AND EVENTS...

_____

_____

_____

_____

_____

_____

_____

_____

_____

DATE: _____ TIME: _____

WEATHER: _____

TODAY I FEEL...

_____
_____
_____
_____

I AM EXCITED ABOUT...

_____
_____
_____
_____

I AM CONCERNED ABOUT...

_____
_____
_____
_____

SOMETHING OR SOMEONE THAT BRIGHTENED MY DAY...

WHAT HAPPENED TODAY...

_____
_____
_____
_____
_____

WHAT I MISS MOST...

_____
_____
_____
_____

THINGS I CAN'T WAIT TO SHARE...

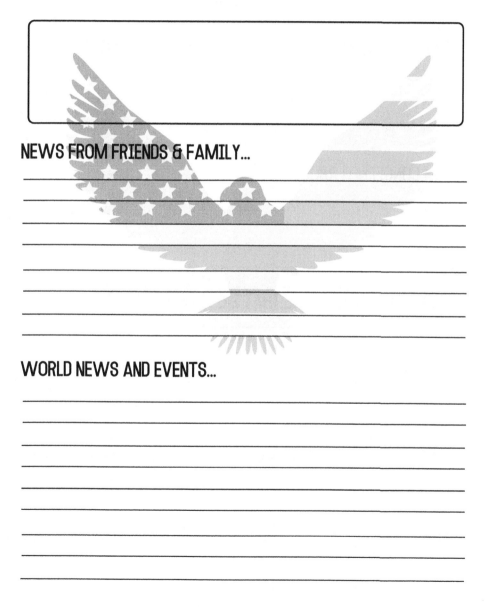

NEWS FROM FRIENDS & FAMILY...

_____
_____
_____
_____
_____
_____
_____

WORLD NEWS AND EVENTS...

_____
_____
_____
_____
_____
_____
_____
_____

DATE: _____   TIME: _____

WEATHER: _____

TODAY I FEEL...

_____
_____
_____
_____

I AM EXCITED ABOUT...

_____
_____
_____

I AM CONCERNED ABOUT...

_____
_____
_____
_____

SOMETHING OR SOMEONE THAT BRIGHTENED MY DAY...

WHAT HAPPENED TODAY...

_____
_____
_____
_____
_____
_____

WHAT I MISS MOST...

_____
_____
_____
_____
_____

THINGS I CAN'T WAIT TO SHARE...

NEWS FROM FRIENDS & FAMILY...

_____
_____
_____
_____
_____
_____
_____

WORLD NEWS AND EVENTS...

_____
_____
_____
_____
_____
_____
_____
_____
_____

DATE: _____ TIME: _____

WEATHER: _____

TODAY I FEEL...

_____
_____
_____
_____

I AM EXCITED ABOUT...

_____
_____
_____
_____

I AM CONCERNED ABOUT...

_____
_____
_____
_____

SOMETHING OR SOMEONE THAT BRIGHTENED MY DAY...

WHAT HAPPENED TODAY...

_____
_____
_____
_____
_____
_____

WHAT I MISS MOST...

_____
_____
_____
_____

THINGS I CAN'T WAIT TO SHARE...

NEWS FROM FRIENDS & FAMILY...

_____
_____
_____
_____
_____
_____

WORLD NEWS AND EVENTS...

_____
_____
_____
_____
_____
_____
_____
_____

DATE: _____ TIME: _____

WEATHER: _____

TODAY I FEEL...

_____
_____
_____
_____

I AM EXCITED ABOUT...

_____
_____
_____
_____

I AM CONCERNED ABOUT...

_____
_____
_____
_____

SOMETHING OR SOMEONE THAT BRIGHTENED MY DAY...

WHAT HAPPENED TODAY...

_____
_____
_____
_____
_____
_____

WHAT I MISS MOST...

_____
_____
_____
_____

THINGS I CAN'T WAIT TO SHARE...

NEWS FROM FRIENDS & FAMILY...

_____
_____
_____
_____
_____
_____
_____
_____

WORLD NEWS AND EVENTS...

_____
_____
_____
_____
_____
_____
_____
_____
_____
_____

DATE: _____   TIME: _____

WEATHER: _____

TODAY I FEEL...
_____
_____
_____
_____

I AM EXCITED ABOUT...
_____
_____
_____

I AM CONCERNED ABOUT...
_____
_____
_____
_____

SOMETHING OR SOMEONE THAT BRIGHTENED MY DAY...

WHAT HAPPENED TODAY...
_____
_____
_____
_____
_____
_____

WHAT I MISS MOST...

_____
_____
_____
_____

THINGS I CAN'T WAIT TO SHARE...

NEWS FROM FRIENDS & FAMILY...

_____
_____
_____
_____
_____
_____
_____

WORLD NEWS AND EVENTS...

_____
_____
_____
_____
_____
_____
_____
_____
_____

DATE: _____   TIME: _____

WEATHER: _____

TODAY I FEEL...
_____
_____
_____
_____

I AM EXCITED ABOUT...
_____
_____
_____
_____

I AM CONCERNED ABOUT...
_____
_____
_____
_____

SOMETHING OR SOMEONE THAT BRIGHTENED MY DAY...

WHAT HAPPENED TODAY...
_____
_____
_____
_____
_____

WHAT I MISS MOST...

_____
_____
_____
_____

THINGS I CAN'T WAIT TO SHARE...

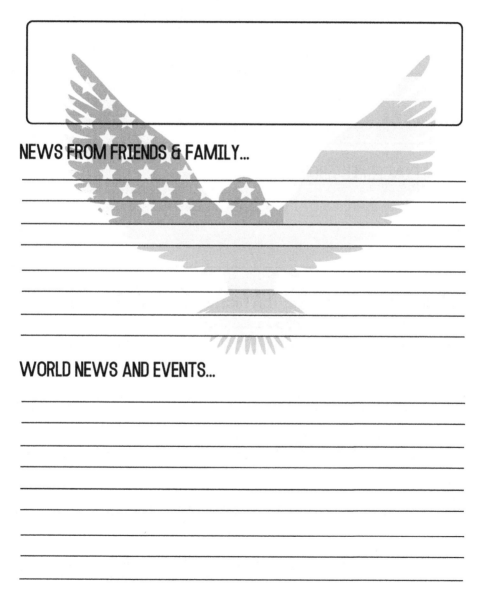

NEWS FROM FRIENDS & FAMILY...

_____
_____
_____
_____
_____
_____
_____

WORLD NEWS AND EVENTS...

_____
_____
_____
_____
_____
_____
_____
_____
_____

DATE: _____   TIME: _____

WEATHER: _____

TODAY I FEEL...

_____
_____
_____
_____

I AM EXCITED ABOUT...

_____
_____
_____
_____

I AM CONCERNED ABOUT...

_____
_____
_____
_____

SOMETHING OR SOMEONE THAT BRIGHTENED MY DAY...

WHAT HAPPENED TODAY...

_____
_____
_____
_____
_____
_____

WHAT I MISS MOST...

_____
_____
_____
_____

THINGS I CAN'T WAIT TO SHARE...

NEWS FROM FRIENDS & FAMILY...

_____
_____
_____
_____
_____
_____
_____

WORLD NEWS AND EVENTS...

_____
_____
_____
_____
_____
_____
_____
_____

DATE: _____ TIME: _____

WEATHER: _____

TODAY I FEEL...
_____
_____
_____
_____

I AM EXCITED ABOUT...
_____
_____
_____

I AM CONCERNED ABOUT...
_____
_____
_____

SOMETHING OR SOMEONE THAT BRIGHTENED MY DAY...

WHAT HAPPENED TODAY...
_____
_____
_____
_____
_____
_____

WHAT I MISS MOST...

_____
_____
_____
_____

THINGS I CAN'T WAIT TO SHARE...

NEWS FROM FRIENDS & FAMILY...

_____
_____
_____
_____
_____
_____

WORLD NEWS AND EVENTS...

_____
_____
_____
_____
_____
_____
_____
_____

DATE: _____ TIME: _____

WEATHER: _____

TODAY I FEEL...

_____
_____
_____
_____

I AM EXCITED ABOUT...

_____
_____
_____
_____

I AM CONCERNED ABOUT...

_____
_____
_____
_____

SOMETHING OR SOMEONE THAT BRIGHTENED MY DAY...

WHAT HAPPENED TODAY...

_____
_____
_____
_____
_____

WHAT I MISS MOST...

THINGS I CAN'T WAIT TO SHARE...

NEWS FROM FRIENDS & FAMILY...

WORLD NEWS AND EVENTS...

DATE: _____ TIME: _____

WEATHER: _____

TODAY I FEEL...

_____
_____
_____
_____

I AM EXCITED ABOUT...

_____
_____
_____
_____

I AM CONCERNED ABOUT...

_____
_____
_____
_____

SOMETHING OR SOMEONE THAT BRIGHTENED MY DAY...

WHAT HAPPENED TODAY...

_____
_____
_____
_____
_____
_____

WHAT I MISS MOST...

_____
_____
_____
_____

THINGS I CAN'T WAIT TO SHARE...

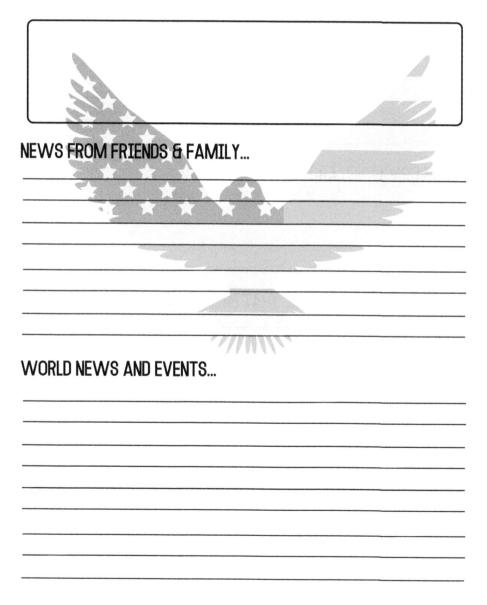

NEWS FROM FRIENDS & FAMILY...

_____
_____
_____
_____
_____
_____

WORLD NEWS AND EVENTS...

_____
_____
_____
_____
_____
_____
_____
_____

DATE: _____ TIME: _____

WEATHER: _____

TODAY I FEEL...

_____
_____
_____

I AM EXCITED ABOUT...

_____
_____
_____

I AM CONCERNED ABOUT...

_____
_____
_____

SOMETHING OR SOMEONE THAT BRIGHTENED MY DAY...

WHAT HAPPENED TODAY...

_____
_____
_____
_____
_____

WHAT I MISS MOST...

_____
_____
_____
_____
_____

THINGS I CAN'T WAIT TO SHARE...

NEWS FROM FRIENDS & FAMILY...

_____
_____
_____
_____
_____
_____
_____
_____

WORLD NEWS AND EVENTS...

_____
_____
_____
_____
_____
_____
_____
_____
_____

DATE: _____ TIME: _____

WEATHER: _____

TODAY I FEEL...

_____
_____
_____
_____

I AM EXCITED ABOUT...

_____
_____
_____
_____

I AM CONCERNED ABOUT...

_____
_____
_____
_____

SOMETHING OR SOMEONE THAT BRIGHTENED MY DAY...

WHAT HAPPENED TODAY...

_____
_____
_____
_____
_____

WHAT I MISS MOST...

THINGS I CAN'T WAIT TO SHARE...

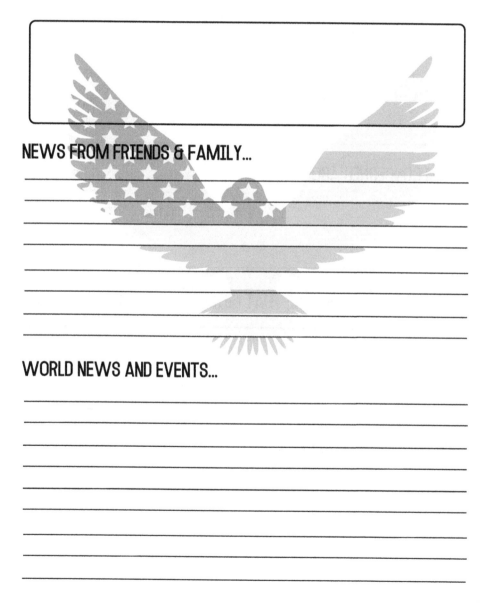

NEWS FROM FRIENDS & FAMILY...

WORLD NEWS AND EVENTS...

DATE: _____   TIME: _____

WEATHER: _____

TODAY I FEEL...

_____
_____
_____
_____

I AM EXCITED ABOUT...

_____
_____
_____
_____

I AM CONCERNED ABOUT...

_____
_____
_____
_____

SOMETHING OR SOMEONE THAT BRIGHTENED MY DAY...

WHAT HAPPENED TODAY...

_____
_____
_____
_____
_____
_____

WHAT I MISS MOST...

_____
_____
_____
_____

THINGS I CAN'T WAIT TO SHARE...

NEWS FROM FRIENDS & FAMILY...

_____
_____
_____
_____
_____
_____
_____

WORLD NEWS AND EVENTS...

_____
_____
_____
_____
_____
_____
_____
_____
_____

DATE: _____ TIME: _____

WEATHER: _____

TODAY I FEEL...
_____
_____
_____
_____

I AM EXCITED ABOUT...
_____
_____
_____

I AM CONCERNED ABOUT...
_____
_____
_____

SOMETHING OR SOMEONE THAT BRIGHTENED MY DAY...
┌───┐
│   │
│   │
│   │
└───┘

WHAT HAPPENED TODAY...
_____
_____
_____
_____
_____

WHAT I MISS MOST...

_____
_____
_____
_____

THINGS I CAN'T WAIT TO SHARE...

NEWS FROM FRIENDS & FAMILY...

_____
_____
_____
_____
_____
_____
_____

WORLD NEWS AND EVENTS...

_____
_____
_____
_____
_____
_____
_____
_____
_____

DATE: _____   TIME: _____

WEATHER: _____

TODAY I FEEL...

_____
_____
_____
_____

I AM EXCITED ABOUT...

_____
_____
_____
_____

I AM CONCERNED ABOUT...

_____
_____
_____
_____

SOMETHING OR SOMEONE THAT BRIGHTENED MY DAY...

WHAT HAPPENED TODAY...

_____
_____
_____
_____
_____
_____

WHAT I MISS MOST...

_____
_____
_____
_____

THINGS I CAN'T WAIT TO SHARE...

NEWS FROM FRIENDS & FAMILY...

_____
_____
_____
_____
_____
_____
_____

WORLD NEWS AND EVENTS...

_____
_____
_____
_____
_____
_____
_____
_____
_____

DATE: _____ TIME: _____

WEATHER: _____

TODAY I FEEL...

_____
_____
_____
_____

I AM EXCITED ABOUT...

_____
_____
_____
_____

I AM CONCERNED ABOUT...

_____
_____
_____
_____

SOMETHING OR SOMEONE THAT BRIGHTENED MY DAY...

WHAT HAPPENED TODAY...

_____
_____
_____
_____
_____
_____

WHAT I MISS MOST...

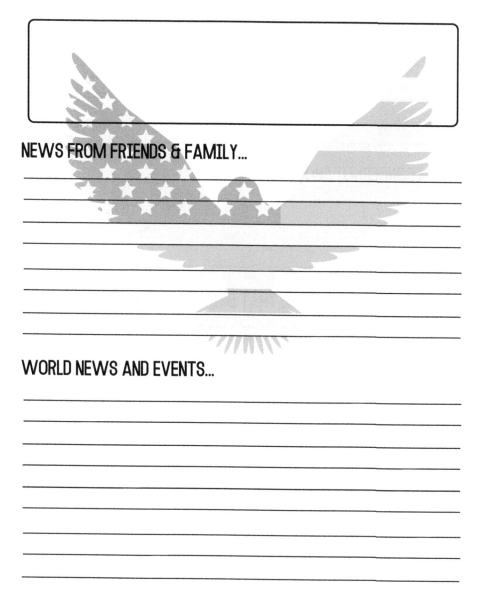

THINGS I CAN'T WAIT TO SHARE...

NEWS FROM FRIENDS & FAMILY...

WORLD NEWS AND EVENTS...

DATE: _____ TIME: _____

WEATHER: _____

TODAY I FEEL...

_____
_____
_____
_____

I AM EXCITED ABOUT...

_____
_____
_____
_____

I AM CONCERNED ABOUT...

_____
_____
_____
_____

SOMETHING OR SOMEONE THAT BRIGHTENED MY DAY...

WHAT HAPPENED TODAY...

_____
_____
_____
_____
_____
_____

WHAT I MISS MOST...

_____
_____
_____
_____

THINGS I CAN'T WAIT TO SHARE...

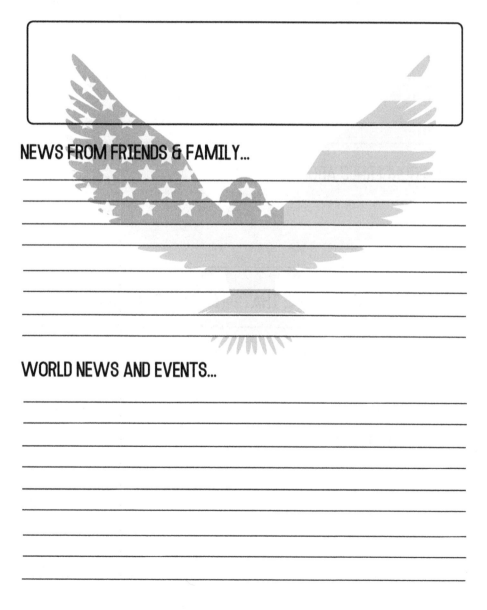

NEWS FROM FRIENDS & FAMILY...

_____
_____
_____
_____
_____
_____
_____

WORLD NEWS AND EVENTS...

_____
_____
_____
_____
_____
_____
_____
_____

DATE: _____ TIME: _____

WEATHER: _____

TODAY I FEEL...

_____
_____
_____
_____

I AM EXCITED ABOUT...

_____
_____
_____
_____

I AM CONCERNED ABOUT...

_____
_____
_____
_____

SOMETHING OR SOMEONE THAT BRIGHTENED MY DAY...

WHAT HAPPENED TODAY...

_____
_____
_____
_____
_____

WHAT I MISS MOST...

_____
_____
_____
_____

THINGS I CAN'T WAIT TO SHARE...

NEWS FROM FRIENDS & FAMILY...

_____
_____
_____
_____
_____
_____

WORLD NEWS AND EVENTS...

_____
_____
_____
_____
_____
_____
_____
_____

DATE: _____ TIME: _____

WEATHER: _____

TODAY I FEEL...

_____
_____
_____
_____

I AM EXCITED ABOUT...

_____
_____
_____
_____

I AM CONCERNED ABOUT...

_____
_____
_____
_____

SOMETHING OR SOMEONE THAT BRIGHTENED MY DAY...

WHAT HAPPENED TODAY...

_____
_____
_____
_____
_____
_____

WHAT I MISS MOST...

_____
_____
_____
_____
_____

THINGS I CAN'T WAIT TO SHARE...

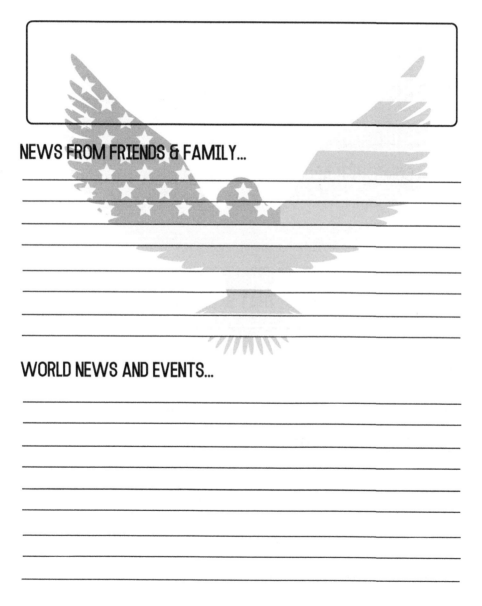

NEWS FROM FRIENDS & FAMILY...

_____
_____
_____
_____
_____
_____
_____
_____

WORLD NEWS AND EVENTS...

_____
_____
_____
_____
_____
_____
_____
_____
_____

DATE: _____ TIME: _____

WEATHER: _____

TODAY I FEEL...

_____
_____
_____
_____

I AM EXCITED ABOUT...

_____
_____
_____
_____

I AM CONCERNED ABOUT...

_____
_____
_____
_____

SOMETHING OR SOMEONE THAT BRIGHTENED MY DAY...

WHAT HAPPENED TODAY...

_____
_____
_____
_____
_____
_____

WHAT I MISS MOST...

_____
_____
_____
_____
_____

THINGS I CAN'T WAIT TO SHARE...

NEWS FROM FRIENDS & FAMILY...

_____
_____
_____
_____
_____
_____
_____

WORLD NEWS AND EVENTS...

_____
_____
_____
_____
_____
_____
_____
_____

DATE: _____ TIME: _____

WEATHER: _____

TODAY I FEEL...

_____
_____
_____
_____

I AM EXCITED ABOUT...

_____
_____
_____
_____

I AM CONCERNED ABOUT...

_____
_____
_____
_____

SOMETHING OR SOMEONE THAT BRIGHTENED MY DAY...

WHAT HAPPENED TODAY...

_____
_____
_____
_____
_____
_____

WHAT I MISS MOST...

_____
_____
_____
_____

THINGS I CAN'T WAIT TO SHARE...

NEWS FROM FRIENDS & FAMILY...

_____
_____
_____
_____
_____
_____
_____

WORLD NEWS AND EVENTS...

_____
_____
_____
_____
_____
_____
_____
_____
_____

DATE: _____ TIME: _____

WEATHER: _____

TODAY I FEEL...

_____
_____
_____
_____

I AM EXCITED ABOUT...

_____
_____
_____

I AM CONCERNED ABOUT...

_____
_____
_____
_____

SOMETHING OR SOMEONE THAT BRIGHTENED MY DAY...

WHAT HAPPENED TODAY...

_____
_____
_____
_____
_____
_____

WHAT I MISS MOST...

_____
_____
_____
_____

THINGS I CAN'T WAIT TO SHARE...

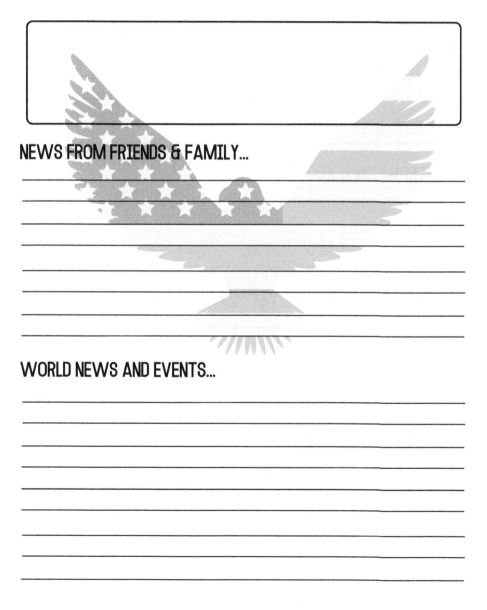

NEWS FROM FRIENDS & FAMILY...

_____
_____
_____
_____
_____
_____
_____

WORLD NEWS AND EVENTS...

_____
_____
_____
_____
_____
_____
_____
_____

DATE: _____   TIME: _____

WEATHER: _____

TODAY I FEEL...
_____
_____
_____
_____

I AM EXCITED ABOUT...
_____
_____
_____

I AM CONCERNED ABOUT...
_____
_____
_____

SOMETHING OR SOMEONE THAT BRIGHTENED MY DAY...

WHAT HAPPENED TODAY...
_____
_____
_____
_____
_____
_____

WHAT I MISS MOST...

_____
_____
_____
_____

THINGS I CAN'T WAIT TO SHARE...

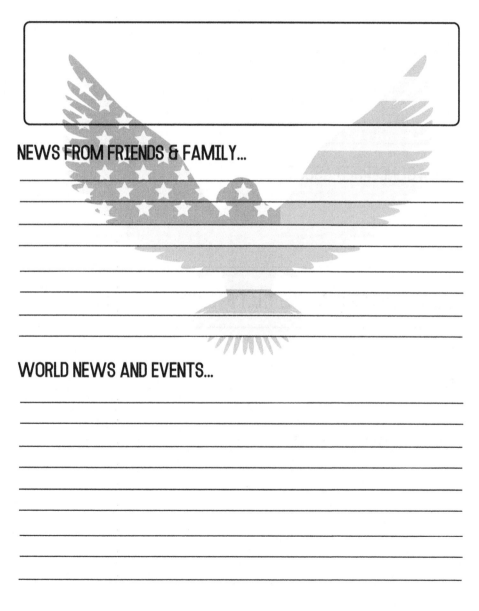

NEWS FROM FRIENDS & FAMILY...

_____
_____
_____
_____
_____
_____

WORLD NEWS AND EVENTS...

_____
_____
_____
_____
_____
_____
_____
_____

DATE: _____   TIME: _____

WEATHER: _____

TODAY I FEEL...
_____
_____
_____
_____

I AM EXCITED ABOUT...
_____
_____
_____
_____

I AM CONCERNED ABOUT...
_____
_____
_____
_____

SOMETHING OR SOMEONE THAT BRIGHTENED MY DAY...

WHAT HAPPENED TODAY...
_____
_____
_____
_____
_____
_____

WHAT I MISS MOST...

_____
_____
_____
_____

THINGS I CAN'T WAIT TO SHARE...

NEWS FROM FRIENDS & FAMILY...

_____
_____
_____
_____
_____
_____
_____

WORLD NEWS AND EVENTS...

_____
_____
_____
_____
_____
_____
_____
_____
_____

DATE: _____   TIME: _____

WEATHER: _____

TODAY I FEEL...

_____
_____
_____
_____

I AM EXCITED ABOUT...

_____
_____
_____

I AM CONCERNED ABOUT...

_____
_____
_____
_____

SOMETHING OR SOMEONE THAT BRIGHTENED MY DAY...

WHAT HAPPENED TODAY...

_____
_____
_____
_____
_____

WHAT I MISS MOST...

_____
_____
_____
_____

THINGS I CAN'T WAIT TO SHARE...

NEWS FROM FRIENDS & FAMILY...

_____
_____
_____
_____
_____
_____
_____

WORLD NEWS AND EVENTS...

_____
_____
_____
_____
_____
_____
_____
_____
_____

DATE: _____   TIME: _____

WEATHER: _____

TODAY I FEEL...
_____
_____
_____
_____

I AM EXCITED ABOUT...
_____
_____
_____
_____

I AM CONCERNED ABOUT...
_____
_____
_____
_____

SOMETHING OR SOMEONE THAT BRIGHTENED MY DAY...

WHAT HAPPENED TODAY...
_____
_____
_____
_____
_____
_____

WHAT I MISS MOST...

_____
_____
_____
_____

THINGS I CAN'T WAIT TO SHARE...

NEWS FROM FRIENDS & FAMILY...

_____
_____
_____
_____
_____
_____
_____

WORLD NEWS AND EVENTS...

_____
_____
_____
_____
_____
_____
_____
_____
_____

DATE: _____ TIME: _____

WEATHER: _____

TODAY I FEEL...

_____
_____
_____
_____
_____

I AM EXCITED ABOUT...

_____
_____
_____
_____

I AM CONCERNED ABOUT...

_____
_____
_____
_____

SOMETHING OR SOMEONE THAT BRIGHTENED MY DAY...

WHAT HAPPENED TODAY...

_____
_____
_____
_____
_____
_____

WHAT I MISS MOST...

THINGS I CAN'T WAIT TO SHARE...

NEWS FROM FRIENDS & FAMILY...

WORLD NEWS AND EVENTS...

Made in the USA
Las Vegas, NV
22 June 2023

73757575R00056